KU-489-246

THE HOW AND WHY WONDER BOOK OF

BIRDS

Written *by* JOHN GOODERS
Illustrated by PETER NAMAN

CORN BUNTING

FEMALE REED BUNTING

TRANSWORLD PUBLISHERS ★ LONDON
A NATIONAL GENERAL COMPANY

BOTH LIFE-SIZE

MALE SPARROW

ROBIN

INTRODUCTION

Many books for beginners are so simple as to be virtually useless. They "talk down" to people who are quite capable of understanding complex ideas provided that they are put over in simple form. Often it is not the ideas that are difficult but the language in which they are expressed. In this book ideas about evolution and adaptation to a way of life are explained so that even quite young people can understand more about the birds that surround them. We are all bird-watchers in some way or another and, being human, if we see something we like to try to understand it.

Birds are becoming more and more attractive to more and more people who find enjoyment and relaxation simply by watching their actions and movements, their colours and skills. But at the very same time the number of birds is getting fewer. Each new action by man involves interfering with the world in which we live—a world that is becoming increasingly difficult for birds to find a place to live in. The only ray of hope is that by understanding birds we will come to care about them and take action in time to stop them disappearing from the face of the Earth.

John Gooders.

Originally published in Great Britain
by Transworld Publishers Ltd.
PRINTING HISTORY
Transworld Edition published 1972
Transworld Edition reprinted 1973
Copyright © 1972 Transworld Publishers Ltd.
All rights reserved.
The How and Why Wonder Book Series is originated
and published in the U.S.A. by Grosset and Dunlap Inc.,
a National General Company.
Published by Transworld Publishers Ltd., 57/59 Uxbridge Road, Ealing, London W.5.
Printed by Purnell & Sons Ltd., Paulton (Somerset) and London.

Contents

BLUE TIT

NEST BOX

EGG

A NEST INSIDE THE BOX

FOSSIL SKELETON (RE-ARRANGED FOR
CLARITY) OF PTERODACTYLUS SCOLOPACICEPS.
THESE FLYING REPTILES INCLUDE THE
PTERANODON, THE LARGEST FLYING ANIMAL
WITH A SPAN OF 27 FEET.

ARCHAEOPTERIX, THE FIRST KNOWN FOSSIL BIRD.

Some of the earliest known birds.

The Beginnings of Birds

The planet on which we live is constantly changing.

The beginnings of birds

At times it gets warmer, at others colder. New land rises from the seas and old land disappears beneath the waves. Parts of the Earth that were once warm and lush are now cold and barren. Along with each change in the environment there are changes in the animals and plants that are best able to survive in the new conditions. It is no accident that huge areas of the northern parts of the world, in Canada and Siberia, are densely covered with a growth of coniferous trees—they are best suited to the short summers and dreadfully cold winters. If suddenly it became warmer they would be gradually replaced by species of plants better suited to the new conditions. As the larches, spruces and pines decline a whole host of birds and animals would decline with them but others would take their place.

Dinosaurs we know only as things of the past. When conditions changed these great lumbering reptiles were unable to survive, and in any future climatic change there will be animals alive today that will disappear.

There are at present some 8,500

4

distinct species of birds alive in the world, but it is calculated that between a half and one and a half million different species have existed in the past.

The remains of the earliest known bird were found in a slate quarry in Bavaria in 1861.

Which was the first bird?

A second skeleton was found in 1877. and a third in 1956. All three birds are thought to be the same species—*Archaeopteryx lithographica*, commonly known as Archaeopteryx, 'the ancient winged animal'.

This bird was remarkably similar to present-day birds, but its skeleton shows close links with the reptiles that were its predecessors. Among other features it had a pronouncedly rep-tilian tail of twenty vertebrae, three well developed claws along the forward edge of each wing, and a rather fearsome array of teeth. But it *was* a bird. It had a developed wish-bone, and was covered with feathers the same as those of the birds of the present day. It could fly, though not as well as many modern birds and with three toes facing forwards and one backwards, the structure of its foot was much the same as most perching birds today.

Bird evolution in the Jurassic and Cretaceous periods was not a very speedy

Did the birds that we know today develop immediately?

process. Cretaceous birds were predominantly seabirds very like modern divers and gulls. Hesperornis is like a

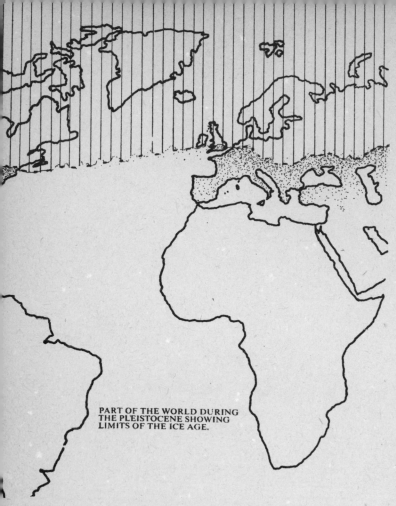

PART OF THE WORLD DURING THE PLEISTOCENE SHOWING LIMITS OF THE ICE AGE.

The world in the Ice Age.

American Eocene.

The Pleistocene, some two million years ago, saw the beginning of the phenomenal Ice

Why did birds that had previously existed successfully finally disappear?

Age. Periods of severe icing of the Earth's surface, when much of the land was covered with glaciers similar to the Antarctic today, alternated with milder periods. The severity of the climate spelt extinction for many families of birds that had previously survived millions of years. And the gradual withdrawal of the Wurm Ice Age, a mere 10,000 years ago, still has remarkable effects on the distribution of many birds today.

Several birds have a broken distribution in Siberia showing that they have not finished spreading back into areas that were previously uninhabited because of ice. Some duck and geese, for example, continued to breed on the verge of extinction, only at a few oases of vegetation among a sea of ice. As the ice retreated they expanded their ranges but still have not fully occupied all of the suitable habitat today.

Other birds that have occupied all suitable areas still maintain migra-

Does the Ice Age still affect birds that have spread back into suitable lands?

tional habits established during the period when Europe was under ice. The blackcap for example migrates south-westwards from Spain, France, Germany and Denmark but south-eastwards from Austria, Hungary and Poland. This migrational-divide, as it is called, indicates that blackcaps were once divided into two breeding areas with two distinct migration routes that have been maintained ever since.

huge great northern diver but with a formidable fish-gripping row of teeth.

During the great Eocene period Europe and America enjoyed a tropical climate that saw the decline of the monsters and a growth in the number and distribution of birds including many belonging to families still in existence today. Albatross, penguin, crane, flamingo, curlew and kingfisher can all be found fossilized in rocks dating back to the Eocene period. Evolution continued apace through the Oligocene, Miocene and Pliocene with more and more modern families appearing. Though blind alleys were persistently taken they did not produce the outrageous forms like the huge flightless *Diatryma Steini* of the North

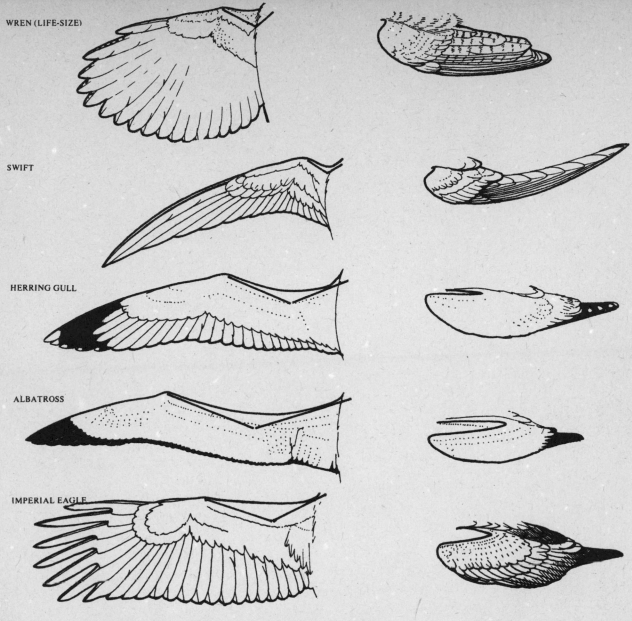

WREN (LIFE-SIZE)

SWIFT

HERRING GULL

ALBATROSS

IMPERIAL EAGLE

Birds' wings are different shapes as they are adapted to suit living conditions.

Flight and the Structure of Birds

Birds vary in size from the huge ostrich to the minute hummingbirds.

Birds look different but do they differ in other ways too?

They are differently shaped, they have different shaped bills, their legs can be as long as the flamingo or as short as the swift. Some are vivid bright colours others are dull camouflaged browns and greens. They live from mountain tops to sea level and below. Some swim and dive for their food, others dig into mud-banks, and many find all they need in the air. Birds like the red grouse stay all their life in the area where they were born; others like the Arctic tern cover thousands of miles each year migrating from the cold north of the Arctic to the equally cold Antarctic. But birds do have one thing in common—flight.

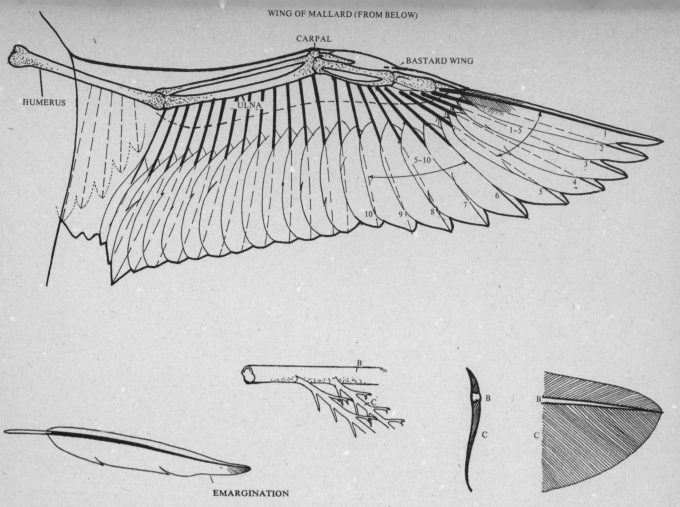

Diagrams showing the bone structure of a wing; and a feather as seen through a magnifying glass.

The ostrich, and many other birds,

Can all birds fly?

rely not on flight but on walking, running or hiding to escape their enemies. But all birds can either fly or they have evolved from other species that could fly. The vast majority of birds can fly and their physical structure is adapted to flight in various ways. Most important are the changes that have turned the arm into a wing. All of the bones that make up the human arm can be found in a bird's wing—though several of them have become fused together. Birds have a wrist and an elbow just like humans. If we tried to fly with wings attached to our arms we would expect to develop very powerful arm muscles.

It is a surprise that there is so little muscle on a bird's wing—everyone prefers a chicken leg to a wing with their Christmas dinner. The powerful flight muscles are in fact mounted on the bird's breast on either side of the specially developed keel—or breast bone—the best meat on a chicken. These huge and heavy muscles pull the wing downwards in forceful strokes propelling the bird along.

Feathers probably evolved from the

Why do birds have feathers?

scales of birds' ancestors—the reptiles. The flight feathers on wings and tail are strong stiff structures and yet are 'as light as a feather'. Look at a wing feather under a magnifying glass and you will see the incredibly complex arrangement of barbs, barbules and barbicels that bind the whole structure

8

together. Feathers are light, strong and flexible, all highly necessary qualities for controlled flight. Before aircraft take off the passenger's luggage is carefully weighed and stowed so that weight is evenly distributed. Every pound has to be added up so that the aircraft can fly efficiently. With the flying bird weight is just as important, but it is not pounds but tiny fractions of ounces that are crucial. In animals that live on the land bones are solid heavy structures. Birds cannot afford such luxuries, their bones are thin and filled with a honeycomb for strength and lightness.

The Variety of Birds

If an ornithologist was given a bird that he had never seen or heard of before he would be able to build up a remarkable picture of how it lived merely by examining its anatomy. The size, shape and structure of its bill and legs and feet in particular would be able to tell him a considerable amount about the bird.

Most small perching birds have three toes pointing forwards and one backwards. Woodpeckers who spend their lives climbing trees, however, have two toes forward and two back, while swifts, who spend almost their entire life in the air, have all four toes capable of

Why do birds' feet vary so much?

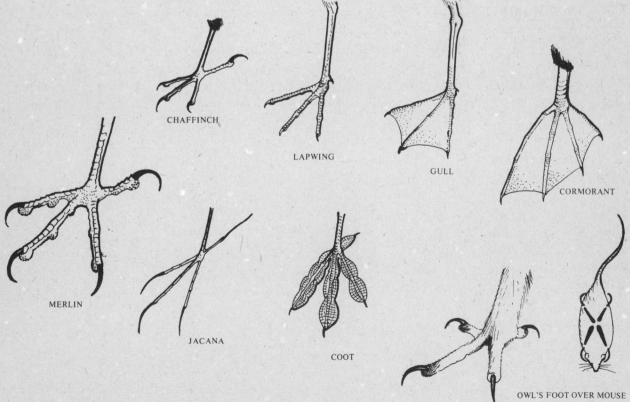

CHAFFINCH

LAPWING

GULL

CORMORANT

MERLIN

JACANA

COOT

OWL'S FOOT OVER MOUSE

Different types of birds' feet:- Lapwing—walking; Chaffinch—perching; Jacana—lily-trotting; Long-eared Owl—grasping; Gull—swimming; Coot—swimming; Merlin—gripping.

pointing forward to cling to the entrance to their nest hole. The swift's legs are short and weak whereas those of an eagle, used for catching and killing prey, are huge, strong and sharp taloned. Ducks have webbed feet suitable for swimming while the Jacana, or lily trotter, has very long toes to spread its weight over a large surface like the snow shoes that men wear when walking on soft snow. The ostrich has only two toes forming a cloven hoof similar to that of domestic cattle and ideally suited to running. But when it comes to legs there is nothing to compare with the inside-leg measurement of the flamingo. Because of its enormous height the flamingo also has to have a very long neck to reach to water level for its

food—but it does enable the birds to feed in very deep water without having to resort to swimming and diving.

If birds' legs are odd enough their bills are often quite incredible.

Why do birds have such a variety of different bill shapes?

The great sweep of the curlew's bill seems strangely grotesque as the bird flies overhead, but on the mud banks it can probe deeper than any other wader and catch prey that hides up to 8 inches below the surface. In contrast the hawfinch has a short, powerful stubby bill that is ideally suited to cracking nuts like the cherry stones of which it is so fond. Between these two extremes is a whole variety of shapes

HAWFINCH   SWIFT   NIGHTJAR   GREEN WOODPECKER

CROSSBILL   GOLDEN EAGLE   DARTER

HYACINTH MACAW   PELICAN   HORNBILL

There are a wide variety of bill shapes suited to different types of feeding requirements.

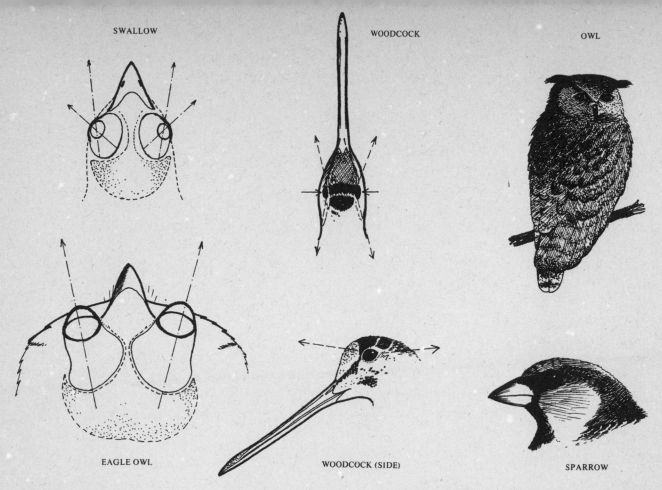

EAGLE OWL   WOODCOCK (SIDE)   SPARROW

The position of a bird's eyes depends on its manner of living. A Swallow has excellent binocular vision; a Woodcock sees as well behind as in front; and the Eagle Owl sees only in front where its prey is found.

and sizes suited to different methods of feeding. Nightjars and swifts have tiny little bills but huge great mouths to gather the flies and moths that they feed on in flight. Woodpeckers have chisel-like bills used to break away the bark of trees in search of grubs; darters have dagger-like rapiers for spearing fish; golden eagles massive flesh tearing bills and crossbills a peculiar over-lapping bill for extracting the seeds from hard pine cones.

Eyesight is another well developed clue to a bird's manner of living. Owls, and to a lesser extent other predators, have eyes at the front of their head giving them excellent binocular vision like humans, but a very small field of view. Owls

Can birds see behind them?

have overcome this by being able to turn their heads completely round so that they are facing the exact opposite direction of their bodies. Birds that are preyed upon on the other hand need to keep a careful watch for their enemies and have eyes at the sides of their heads so that they can see danger even when it is behind them. The eyesight of birds is much more acute than that of man and you can be reasonably certain that if you can see the bird it can see you far better. These then are some of the ways that birds are adapted to the environment in which they live. Just as they are helpful clues to the ornithologist trying to discover how a bird lives, they are also useful to the bird-watcher trying to identify a bird that he has found.

11

GOLDEN EAGLE (IN MOUNTAINS)

LITTLE TERN (SEASHORE)

DIPPER (FAST-FLOWING STREAMS)

SWIFT (IN THE AIR)

Where a bird lives is important for identification.

Bird Identification

Identification is one of the most important skills that anyone interested in birds can develop. It is of little use to say that a small greyish bird was seen at a locality where it does not usually occur. Whereas if the bird is correctly identified as a rock pipit the observation will add something to your knowledge and may increase our understanding of the pipit's life.

Why is naming the birds important?

Putting a name to a bird is often a difficult and painstaking job. But there are certain things to watch out for. Size is

How does one learn to identify birds?

a useful guide and is best expressed as a comparison with species with which one is already familiar—like smaller than a sparrow, larger than a thrush, and so on. Careful notes should be made of the size and shape of the bill and the length and colour of the legs. Here too comparison is more useful than vague terms like long, quite long and short. The best method is to compare the length of bill with the length of the head, and note whether or not the legs trail behind the tail when the bird flies.

Size and colour are often not enough. What a bird does and where it is seen are very important. If it is seen swimming your search for a name can take

BITTERN (IN REEDS)

GREEN WOODPECKER (IN TREES)

Can birds be identified as they fly past?

Many birds have very characteristic methods of flying. Fulmars and shearwaters have long narrow wings like gliders and rely on eddies of wind along the edge of waves to give them lift and keep them airborne. Their larger relatives the albatrosses are so dependent on a strong wind that a flat calm stops them flying altogether. These birds skim low over the sea with a few flaps and long glides. Buzzards, eagles and vultures too depend on the air rather than their own efforts to keep them aloft. But in their case it is not wind but thermals—hot air rising from land warmed by the heat of the Sun. On a fine sunny day these birds of prey will circle round and round rising high in the sky, almost as fast as the hot air around them, without so much as a single flap of their broad wings. If they want to go somewhere they rise right out of sight before gliding off to a favoured feeding ground or another thermal where they can gain height once more.

Most birds, however, flap their wings. Swallows have a fast jiggling flight; woodpeckers a rythmic undulating one. Kestrels, often wrongly called sparrowhawks, hover over the fields, while terns hover and plunge into lakes and the sea. Wheatears fly over very open country moving from one prominent perch on a rock or post to the next, whereas willow warblers flit among the leaves of a tree or bush. Each bird has something of its own but the difficulty comes not in separating say a duck from a bunting, but in separating one duck from another duck. All of the things to watch for already mentioned must be carefully noted and after a while the sorts of birds to be expected in different types of landscape will become well known,

one course, if it is feeding on the sea-shore another, and if it flits about in trees or bushes yet another. A striped brown bird on a garden lawn might be a dunnock, in a bed of reeds a sedge warbler, and climbing in woodland a tree-creeper. Even the type of tree can be a help. Coniferous forests hold coal tits and black grouse which are seldom found in deciduous woods. What does the bird do and where was it seen must be carefully noted. Was it seen with other birds? Were they the same or different birds? How many were there? Only when these basic points have been noted is it possible to get down to the bird itself and ask how it flew and what colour it was.

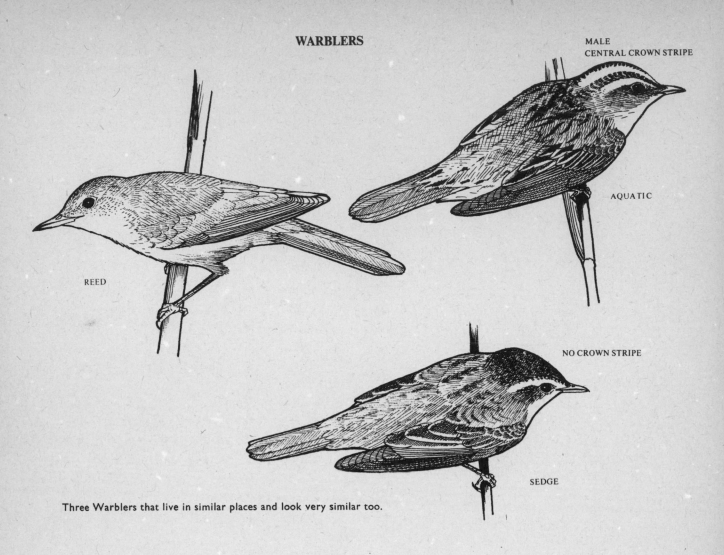

MALE
CENTRAL CROWN STRIPE

AQUATIC

REED

NO CROWN STRIPE

SEDGE

Three Warblers that live in similar places and look very similar too.

and eventually second nature.

Plumage colouration has been left to last because it is one of the most

Is a bird's colour of no importance?

valuable guides to bird recognition. Given two birds that are found in the same sort of places, feed in similar ways, are roughly the same size and fly in the same manner, plumage differences are the real key. But here too there is an important warning. Supposing you have discovered a bird, smaller than a sparrow, on its own flitting among a lot of reeds and flying only short distances before disappearing again. It could be any one of a number of different species. Next time it comes to the top of a

reed you notice that it is brown above and buff below. Referring to your identification book still leaves you several highly confusing birds to choose from. Only when you have carefully noted that the back is streaked brown and dark and that it has a prominent stripe above the eye can you be reasonably certain that it is a sedge and not a reed warbler. Even then there are several less likely birds that you could confuse with it.

Even more confusing are birds that are so similar that they can only be

Are there birds that even the experts cannot tell apart?

distinguished by their songs. The chiffchaff and willow warbler, for example, look almost identical, though the willow warbler often, but not always, has light brownish legs. Both are little greenish birds, live in woods, are summer visitors to northern Europe and feed and behave in the same way. Yet while the willow warbler sings a sweet little trill, the chiffchaff says 'chiff-chaff chiff-chaff' endlessly. Fortunately most birds are much easier to distinguish than these.

Many birds have useful marks that

What is a 'field mark'?

are a sure guide to identification if spotted. Bars on the wings, usually white, are particularly important among waders and duck. Tail patterns also help identify waders as well as swallows and wheatears. Stripes on the head and bars on the folded wing are often crucial in identifying some small warblers. These are the things to look for and note.

Field notes on any bird that cannot

How should I set out my field notes?

be identified on the spot should be set out under the following headings:
Date: Place: Type of vegetation:
Time: Weather conditions:
Size: (compared with sparrow or blackbird):
Bill length: Leg length: Leg colour:
Plumage description:
Field marks:
Call or song:
What did it do:
How did it fly:
How did it feed:
How many were there:
Other species present:
Remarks:
Identification:
Note—be prepared to leave the space for identification blank if you are still not sure what the bird was.

Where Birds Live

Birds are built in different ways to fit

What happens to birds if the area where they live changes?

them for their habitat. If the habitat changes either the bird changes or it becomes extinct. Almost every niche of the world's surface is utilized by some form of bird life. The more productive of life the environment, the greater number and variety of birds it is able to support.

Some birds are highly adaptable. They can adjust to new environments quite quickly and take advantage of new sources of food and new places to live. Others are very set in their ways and are unable to change. Destroy all the reed beds and the reed warbler would disappear whereas the more varied habitat of the sedge warbler would enable it to adjust to the changing situation. A few birds only manage to exist at all because of a constantly changing environment. The tiny Kirtland's warbler for instance lives only in American forests that have been destroyed by fires. Because man has taken control of the forests and takes every step to prevent fires Kirtland's warbler has been severely reduced in numbers. To conserve the species naturalists have purchased over 4000 acres which are systematically burnt and planted to ensure a place for the warbler to live and breed.

SNOW FINCH

BLACK
REDSTART

ROCK
THRUSH

ROCK PARTRIDGE

ALPINE CHOUGHS

NUTCRACKER

CRESTED TIT

FIRECREST

RED-BACKED SHRIKE

REDSTART

BONELLI'S WARBLER

Alpine Zones: at different heights one finds different birds suited to different modes of life.

The study of the relationship between an animal and its environment is

What is ecology?

called ecology an understanding of which is important to anyone interested in birds. Ultimately all animals rely on the food produced by plants.

Many insect larvae turn into flies in water and emerge to the surface. At times of hatching flies are sometimes incredibly numerous and provide a huge food supply for trout and other fish. But they are also food to the black tern which picks them delicately

Who eats who?

from the surface. The trout are, in turn, preyed upon by larger fish like pike and birds like the osprey which plunges talons first into the water. But the osprey also takes pike and the pike also eats young birds like duck and moorhen. These relationships show the complexity of the "who eats who" of ecology. And the ornithologist studying the osprey is hard put to sort out the factors that control the numbers of birds that any particular lake can maintain.

Mountain ranges are excellent places to study the ways in which birds fit into their environment. In Switzerland one can walk up a mountain side through a wide variety of habitats seeing different birds all the way. In the hay meadows along the valley floor redstarts, Bonelli's warblers and red-backed

Do the birds one finds vary according to altitude?

shrikes are the most numerous birds. As the hillside gets steeper the pine forests begin and nutcrackers, crested tits and firecrests are dominant. Higher up still conditions become more severe and the pines do not grow as densely or strongly. Among the scattered trees rock partridges find their food and nest among the boulders, and citril finches sing from the stunted trees. Above the tree-line, the upper limit beyond which trees will not grow at all, Alpine choughs, rock thrushes and black redstarts, close relatives of the redstarts we left 6000 feet below in the valley, become most numerous. Nearer the top only Alpine accentors can eke out a living, while the top of the mountain itself is the only home of the snow finch. These zones are never clear cut, each gradually merges into the next, but each species of bird has its own ecological niche where it is best able to survive.

17

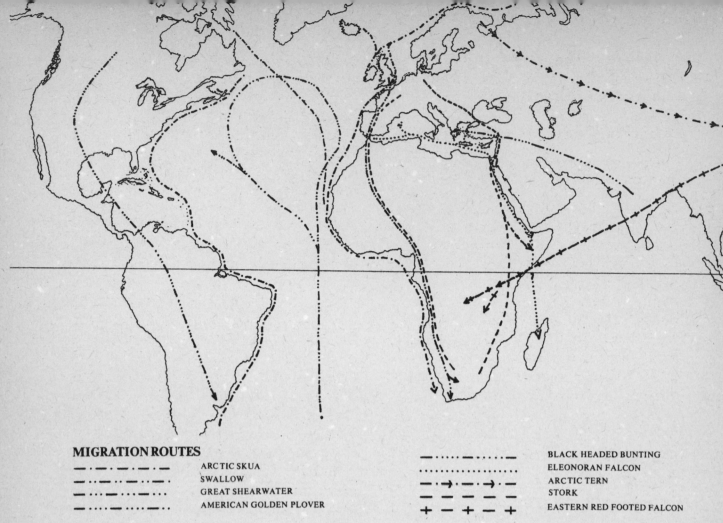

MIGRATION ROUTES

— · — · — · — ARCTIC SKUA
— · · — · · — · · SWALLOW
— · · · — · · · — GREAT SHEARWATER
— · · · · — · · · · AMERICAN GOLDEN PLOVER

— · — — · — — BLACK HEADED BUNTING
· · · · · · · · · · · · ELEONORAN FALCON
— · → · — · → · — ARCTIC TERN
— — — — — — STORK
+ — + — + EASTERN RED FOOTED FALCON

Migration

Why do birds migrate?
Each year the climate of the Earth changes in a regular cycle —spring follows winter and autumn follows summer. Each spring huge areas of the globe are left free of ice and snow for a few brief months of summer. In autumn the snow returns and only the hardiest of animals can survive. During this brief summer beyond the Arctic Circle it is daylight 24 hours each day and plants and insects that have lain dormant through the long and bitter winter burst into life while they can. Mammals emerge from hibernation to breed quickly before the snows come again, and trees a few feet high but tens of years old manage to flower and seed. Though few birds are able to survive in these latitudes all the year round it is not surprising that the abundance of life in the summer has been taken advantage of by millions of birds who leave for milder climates during the winter. Further south in the woodland belts, and even in countries that we consider to be hot even in winter, there is more life in summer than there is in winter, and birds take advantage of any food supply.

Because they can fly birds are highly mobile and the greatest of all migrants, they make long journeys to enjoy a breeding season in the north before heading southwards to spend another summer during our winter. While it appears that they have the best of both worlds the migration journey is highly risky and dangerous. Many millions of birds are killed every year as they stream southward in the autumn and northward in the spring.

For a long time it was thought that some birds migrated during the day and other species did so at night.

Do birds migrate during the day or night?

We now know that sharp divisions of this sort are not appropriate to birds. Many warblers and chats set off on migration at dusk and fly through the night. Sometimes they alight at dawn but at other times they continue to fly right through the next day. Other birds like skylarks and the finches set off at dawn and can be seen migrating during the hours of daylight.

It has always been a puzzle as to how birds find their way on these long journeys. A

How do birds find their way?

swallow will return to the same barn to breed year after year finding its nest after two journeys each of 5000 miles.

Sailors navigate only with the help of a compass and experiments have shown that birds too must have a similar built-in piece of equipment that tells them in which direction to fly. Even with a compass, however, a sailor is unable to pinpoint his position. He must also have a map, an accurate watch and a sextant to confirm his position by the Sun or stars. Migratory birds also navigate by the Sun and stars. On clear evenings when all the stars can be clearly seen birds pass overhead without hindrance to their travels. If, however, the sky clouds over so that their star sign-posts are hidden the birds will come to land at first light which is fine if they are flying over the land but disastrous if they are over the sea. On occasions like this disorientated birds will pick out and head for any ship or landmark. The long powerful beams of lighthouses attract birds for miles around and in cloudy misty weather thousands of birds have been killed by flying into the glass of the lantern.

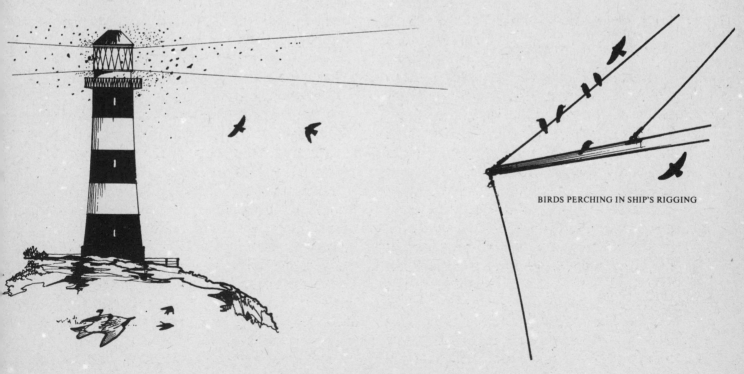

BIRDS PERCHING IN SHIP'S RIGGING

When the sky clouds over birds are attracted to other powerful lights.

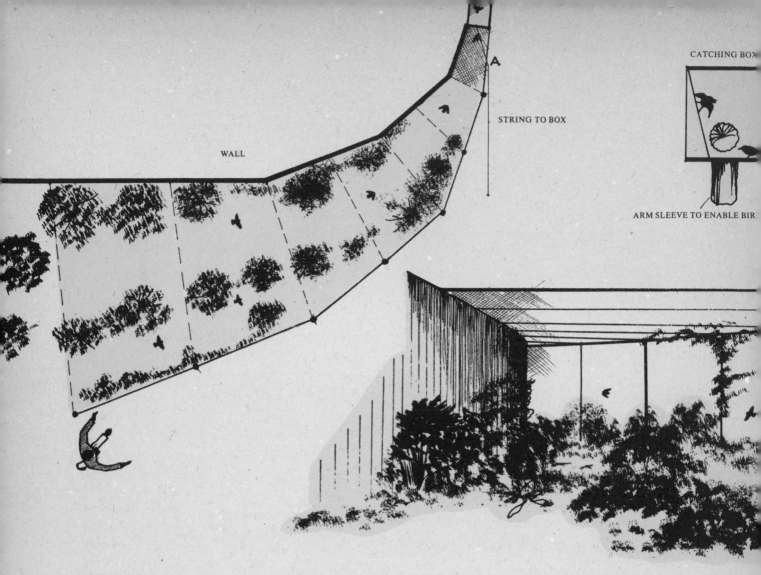

CATCHING BOX

STRING TO BOX

WALL

A

ARM SLEEVE TO ENABLE BIR

Heligoland Traps of fine-mesh wire are used to catch birds at migration concentration points, for example, the bird observatories.

This slaughter can be reduced by illuminating the lighthouse itself so that the birds can see the danger and not just be blinded by the powerful light. Bird protectionists have paid for the installation of these safety lights with the cooperation of the lighthouse management.

If birds are unable to find their way **and they are** over the sea their eventual arrival

What is a "fall" of migrants?

at land will precipitate a "fall"—a huge number of migrants suddenly arriving at a single locality. These falls have long been known to ornithologists who have established bird observatories at the most likely spots on the coast to study migrants. The best sites for an observatory are small isolated islands because when birds are lost at sea the island will attract them from all directions. Peninsulars on the mainland are the next best sites. Though they do not have the pulling power of an island their position enables them to attract birds that are following the coastline during the daytime.

The best examples of observatories are **the island of Heligoland off the coast of**

What is a bird observatory?

Germany and Rybatschi on the Baltic Coast of the Soviet Union. Heligoland

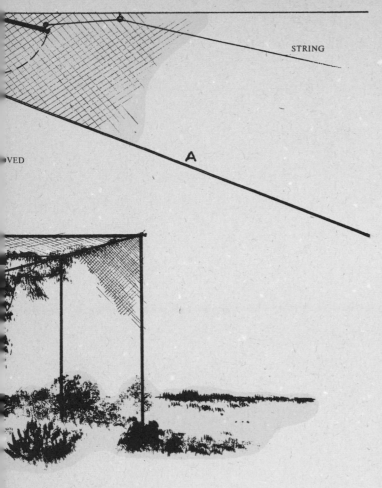

STRING

VED

A

separates the Kurisches Haff from the Baltic Sea. Incredible numbers of birds cross Russia westwards to follow the Baltic coastline and huge numbers come to land and are caught and ringed.

Most of the birds that migrate **southward in autumn are only a** few months old. They do not follow their parents to find the way but set off on their own, relying entirely on their sense of direction, often well in advance of the older more experienced birds. Sometimes things go wrong. It is easy to see that birds travelling westwards to Ireland could meet bad weather and continue out into the Atlantic Ocean.

Do the older birds show the young ones the way?

Sometimes birds get totally **lost and appear in places** hundreds or even thousands of miles from their usual home. These vagrants, as they are called, are a great source of interest adding excitement to the ornithologist's more routine work. In North America vast numbers of birds migrate over the sea between the Canadian border region and Florida and the West Indies. Some even fly direct to South America. If some of these birds get lost they may continue flying over the sea or get lifts on ships to Europe. Some very strange birds are found in the British Isles every year in this way. Birds from the Far East also get lost and wander right across Asia and Europe to Britain and other places. It is curious but sometimes two birds may be seen on the same day, one of which has flown eastward and one westward almost around the world.

Do migrating birds ever get completely lost?

is small, isolated and on the main migration route of birds leaving Scandinavia. In the 1870s a German ornithologist called Gätke started a bird observatory in the island's only large garden and soon birds were being trapped and ringed to discover where they came from and where they were going.

The huge funnel traps devised for **catching the birds have been** imitated all over the world though they are still referred to as "Heligoland" traps. *Rybatschi* is situated on the seventy miles long sand bar that

What is a "Heligoland" trap?

Because of the nature of their flight

Why do eagles and storks appear in flocks on migration?

birds like hawks and storks are unsuited to flapping their wings for long distances. Instead they depend on hot air rising from the land in thermals when it is heated by the warmth of the Sun. As these thermals do not develop over the sea, hawks and storks avoid long sea crossings by concentrating over narrow straights. In Europe such concentrations occur at Falsterbo in southern Sweden, Gibraltar in southern Spain and at the Bosphorus, the straits between the Mediterranean and Black Sea. Every year thousands of birds soar over the land to gain height before gliding across the narrow seas. They form a marvellous spectacle that is mentioned in the Bible and which still attracts ornithologists today.

Seabirds are the longest travellers of all. The Arctic tern breeds as far

Which birds travel the longest distances?

north as there is land and migrates southwards to the limits of the Antarctic pack ice, covering some 22,000 miles each year on migration alone. Add in the daily feeding flights and these birds must cover at least twice as many miles in a year as a hard driven motor car. The Manx shearwater regularly crosses the Atlantic to winter off the coast of Argentina, but one of these birds became the long distance migrant of all time. It was ringed on the island of Skokholm off the coast of Wales and later recovered dead on the coast of Australia.

Mist nets catch birds safely for ringing, weighing and measuring. Only trained scientists may use them.

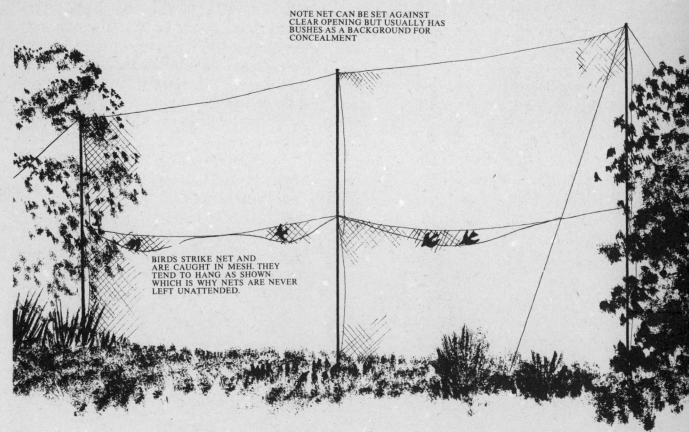

NOTE NET CAN BE SET AGAINST CLEAR OPENING BUT USUALLY HAS BUSHES AS A BACKGROUND FOR CONCEALMENT

BIRDS STRIKE NET AND ARE CAUGHT IN MESH. THEY TEND TO HANG AS SHOWN WHICH IS WHY NETS ARE NEVER LEFT UNATTENDED.

We know so much about bird migration mainly through the scientific study of ringing. A ring of metal alloy is placed on the leg of each bird. Each ring bears a serial number that identifies the bird as an individual and an address for the finder to write to. In this way the movements of a single bird can be followed, as well as telling us how long the bird has lived since ringing.

What is bird-ringing?

Heligoland traps are useful at places where large numbers of birds congregate on migration but they are very expensive to construct and are of little use outside a few localities and a few months of the year. There are all sorts of other

How are birds caught for ringing?

traps that are better for different places and seasons, but by far the most flexible as well as the most effective are mist-nets. Originally imported from Japan where they are used to catch birds for sale, these very fine dark terylene nets are now sold only to fully qualified and licensed ringers. Correctly set they disappear against any dark background and are then invisible to any flying bird. The bird hits the soft net and is neatly pocketed by one of the shelf strings that holds the net in place. Most birds are easy to remove though some species like blue tits that are used to clambering about upside down can end up in a bit of a tangle. But an experienced ringer can soon extract even these birds.

The rate at which birds are recovered varies according to the size and conspicuousness of the species. A large white bird that lives in areas frequented by man stands a better chance of being found than a small brown one that lives in un-inhabited forests. Less than one in a hundred of most small birds are ever heard of again once they have been ringed and released, whereas as many as one in three swans are recovered.

How many birds are found with rings on?

As the chances of recovering a small bird are so slight it is not surprising that ornithologists try to find out as much as possible from the bird while it is in their hands. Observatories and ringers now follow a standard procedure of weighing, ringing, measuring, ageing and sexing, and noting the extent of moult of every bird caught prior to release. Weighing a bird can tell whether it has flown a long way or whether it has been in the area for some time. Like cars, birds use up fuel travelling, but in their case it is stored in

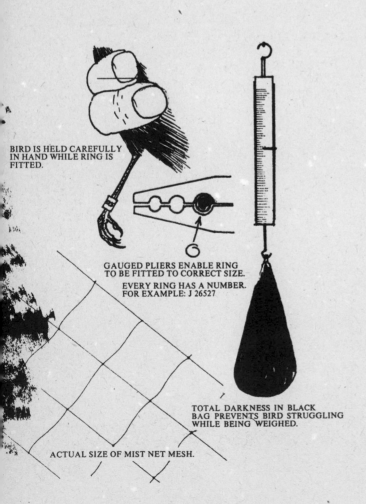

BIRD IS HELD CAREFULLY IN HAND WHILE RING IS FITTED.

GAUGED PLIERS ENABLE RING TO BE FITTED TO CORRECT SIZE.
EVERY RING HAS A NUMBER. FOR EXAMPLE: J 26527

TOTAL DARKNESS IN BLACK BAG PREVENTS BIRD STRUGGLING WHILE BEING WEIGHED.

ACTUAL SIZE OF MIST NET MESH.

the form of fat. Some small birds almost double their normal weight prior to migration. Birds are measured because many species vary in size geographically. Wheatears from Greenland, for instance, have longer wings than those from Europe and are recognised as a separate and distinct sub-species. Though both male and female willow warblers look the same the males, on average, have longer wings than the females and it has been discovered that they have separate migration periods. All of this information adds up to a constantly increasing knowledge and understanding of birds' lives.

MALE BLACKBIRDS IN AGGRESIVE DISPLAY

Blackbirds fighting at the boundaries of their territories.

Courtship and Breeding

Every spring birds leave the flocks in which they have spent the winter and establish themselves in their breeding areas. A great many of them spread out over the countryside by establishing a territory from which they drive all

What is a bird's territory?

other members of their species. Thus a male blackbird will establish a small area inside which he is the king and from which he will chase all other blackbirds—though he will tolerate house sparrows and others whose territories may well overlap. The major requirements of a territory are a nest site and preferably an alternative site, several song posts and, with many small birds, an adequate supply of food.

Having established a territory the male robin, for instance, advertises his presence by singing.

How do birds defend their territories?

This serves to warn intruding males that he owns the land and also to attract a mate. A wandering male receives an elaborate display of aggression and usually beats a hasty retreat. Only when an intruder does not leave do fights develop, and even then it is usually the territory owner that is victorious. The boundaries of the territory are very sharply defined and neighbouring males know exactly how far they can or cannot go without provoking the other. These boundaries are very difficult for us to see though they can be mapped by noting birds' song posts, their nests, where fights occur and by driving a bird until it turns and flies back into its own area.

Though the singing and displaying robin's territory is easy to spot

Do all birds have a territory when they are breeding?

many other birds seem to have no territory at all. Gannets for example nest in huge colonies clustered very closely together. But even here the birds have a territory which they defend against all intruders. A gannet's territory extends as far as it can reach with its beak without leaving the nest. Thus each bird has about a square yard that largely consists of the piled up seaweed of its nest and woe betide any gannet that wanders into the areas between territories. An adult gannet that mistimes its landing will get away with a few pecks as it scrambles to its own

GANNETS

Gannet Colony with closely packed nests.

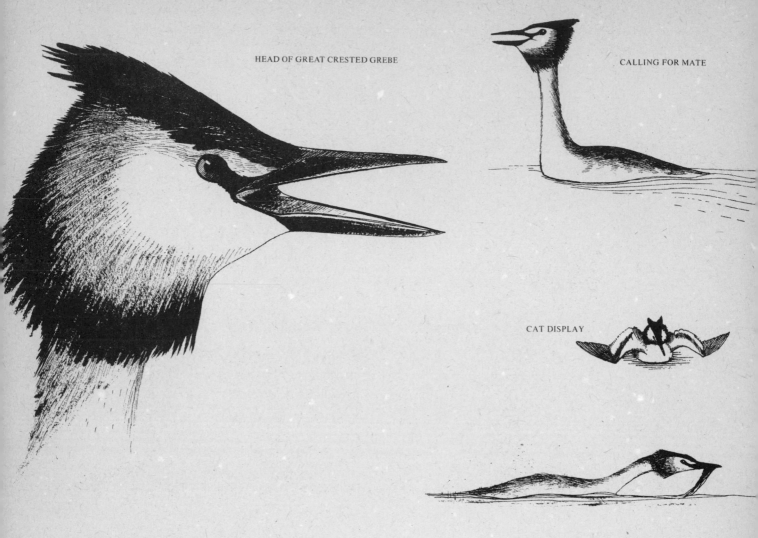

CALLING FOR MATE

CAT DISPLAY

ONE DIVES: BRINGS WEED: AND THEY SWIM TOGETHER

Courtship of the Great Crested Grebe.

domain. A young gannet that wanders away from the nest will be mercilessly pecked to death. Clearly anything that disturbs young gannets is highly dangerous, and an unthinking human may visit a colony determined to do his best for bird protection and leave not knowing that he is responsible for the death of hundreds of young birds.

Having established a territory the male

How do robins recognise one another?

then sets about securing a mate. A hen that wanders into the territory

of a cock robin is treated as an intruder. In the same way as humans are unable to tell male robins from females, so it appears are the robins themselves. Only by adopting a submissive meak posture does the hen robin show the cock that she is not a rival.

Courtship is often a very elaborate

What is bird courtship?

process in birds. Great crested grebes have evolved extremely beautiful plumage with tufts round the head that are shaken vigorously in mutual stimulation designed to bring

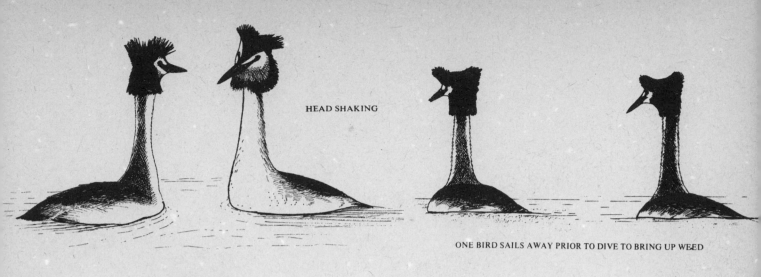

HEAD SHAKING

ONE BIRD SAILS AWAY PRIOR TO DIVE TO BRING UP WEED

ENGUIN DANCE

PENGUIN DANCE ENDS WITH ONE BIRD ASSUMING NORMAL POSITION, AND THE OTHER SLOWLY SINKS (LEFT)

both members of a pair to breeding readiness at the same time. The postures adopted by these birds have been carefully studied and given descriptive names. One in which both members of a pair approach each other with weed held in their bills and rise up from the water close together like dancers is called the 'penguin dance'. In the 'cat display' one bird crouches on the water with wings spread like a cat about to pounce. All of these movements have become rituals that help to stimulate and consolidate the pair bond. Though each species has its own ceremonies they all serve these basic purposes.

Some birds like the cuckoo lay their eggs in the nests of other birds leaving a foster parent to look after incubation and care for the young. The vast majority, however, look after their own offspring—but in an incredible variety of ways. The long-tailed tit constructs a beautiful domed nest of lichens, grasses and hair and lays anything up to 12 eggs. The ringed plover

Why do birds' eggs and nests vary so much?

PENDULUM TIT

LONG-TAILED TIT

EDIBLE SWIFT NEST

GUILLEMOT

GREAT CRESTED GREBE

FAIRY TERN

Birds have a great variety of nests: floating, eg. the Great Crested Grebe; a ball of mosses, eg. the Long-tailed Tit; a hanging chamber, eg. Penduline Tit; no nest at all, eg. the Fairy Tern; a ledge on a cliff, eg. the Guillemot.

does not bother with a nest at all but lays three well camouflaged eggs on the ground, while the guillemot lays a single egg on a bare cliff ledge where one false move sends the egg spinning into the sea hundreds of feet below.

Large birds generally live longer than small birds, and sea birds usually live longer than land birds. As the whole process of breeding is to ensure the continuation of the species, so those that live for the shortest periods must rear more young each year than those that live longer. If the long lived species were to raise many young each year the number of birds would soon be too many for the available food supply and they would perish. Thus the blackbird lays four or five eggs and raises three or more broods in a single summer. If all the

Why do some birds lay one egg and some many times that number?

youngsters survived to the following year there would be six times as many blackbirds as in the previous year and the food supply would be insufficient to enable all the birds to survive let alone breed. Thus the number of eggs is dependent to some extent on the age to which the adults live and the dangers that face them.

The colour of birds' eggs varies according to the way in which they are incubated. Most eggs of birds that nest in holes are white because they do not need to be camouflaged. Whereas those that are laid on the ground are usually browns and greens and harmonise with their surroundings. If, however, the bird itself is camouflaged like the nightjar then the eggs can be quite distinctive because they will never be left uncovered.

Why do bird's eggs vary in colour?

28

The incubation period, that is the length of time taken for the eggs to hatch,

Does the length of time that a bird incubates its eggs vary too?

varies greatly as well. In some of the world's largest birds – albatrosses and vultures – incubation may last several months while the smallest birds sit on their eggs for only a few days before they hatch. For most of the year it is necessary for the adult birds to be covered with feathers as an insulation to maintain their body temperature. But during incubation they need to pass on the heat of their bodies to their young in the eggs. For this reason many birds shed the feathers on their bellies to create a brood patch—an area of bare skin that comes in direct contact with the eggs.

The normal incubation behaviour

CHAFFINCH. MALE FEEDING FEMALE ON NEST

While the mate sits on the eggs during the incubation period, her mate gathers food for her.

involves both cock and hen taking turns to sit on the eggs, though the hen usually plays the larger part. While one bird is sitting the other is away feeding or gathering food for his incubating mate. Small birds like robins change round every couple of hours or so but birds that have to roam further for food, like Manx shearwaters, may be away a couple of days leaving their mate without food for this period. The hen willow warbler has a hard time for as soon as courtship is over the cock loses all interest and leaves the hen to build the nest, perform all the incubation and care for and feed the young totally by herself. A similar system occurs in the phalaropes except that here it is the female who loses interest once the eggs are laid and the drabber male that incubates and looks after the chicks.

Some birds do not incubate at all.

Do all the birds incubate their eggs? Mallee fowl and their relatives build a mound of earth to cover their eggs and the hot Australian sun performs the incubation for them. It is, however, not all idleness for these birds. If the Sun is too hot the eggs will cook unless earth is removed. And the mallee fowl are constantly adjusting the temperature of their natural incubator. Other birds that live in exposed regions in very hot countries have this problem too. Incubation then becomes not a matter of sitting on the eggs to keep them warm but standing over them to create a small area of shade to protect them.

As soon as the young mallee fowl hatch they dig their way to the surface and can run about and fly immediately.

Why do eggs that are laid on the ground take longer to hatch than those in tree nests? But in general the eggs of most birds that nest on the ground take longer to incubate than those laid in safe, well hidden nests in trees, and the young hatch at a more advanced stage of development. Though the ability to fly immediately is highly unusual the young of most ground nests are well feathered and able to walk soon after hatching. This means that they can scatter and hide at the first sign of danger and most of them lie perfectly still relying on their

MOUND ABOUT 15 FEET LONG

MALLEE FOWL BUILDING THE MOUND

YOUNG EMERGING FROM THE MOUND

Mallee fowl building the mound nest.

camouflaged plumage to save them from predators. Young birds in tree nests usually hatch naked, blind and helpless and the major danger here is that while both parents are away the nest is more obvious than while one or the other is incubating.

The white inside of the broken egg shell

Do birds keep their nests clean?

is a conspicuous landmark that the adults get rid of by carrying it away in their bills and dropping well away from the nest. Likewise there is danger of the nest being fouled up by the young bird's droppings, so until they are old enough to evacuate over the side of the nest they produce their waste in a white covered faecal sac on the prompting of an adult who immediately flies off with it to a safe distance. Dead youngsters are removed from the nest for similar reasons. With birds that nest in holes the disposal of egg shells is unimportant and they are usually trampled into the bottom of the nest, but sanitation is equally as important as in open nests and all droppings and dead young are carefully removed.

Though safely hatched the chicks are

When is the most dangerous period in a bird's life?

still faced with the most critical period of their lives. Most birds hatch more eggs than they can ever hope to feed. This provides a safety mechanism that enables them to rear more young if there is an abundant food supply. If, however, food is in restricted supply, as it usually is, then at least one of the brood will starve to death.

Nature is seldom fair. Given a limited amount of food human beings would share it equally. Adult birds, however, do not spread the food they collect among their brood. They feed the most forceful chick with the largest mouth until it is full up before feeding the next. This means that the weakest are trodden under by the strongest. It also means that in a poor season, when food is hard to come by, the adults make every attempt to ensure that at least one of their brood survives to leave the nest rather than none at all, which would happen if the limited food supply was spread evenly among the brood It is this same mechanism that allows the young cuckoo to survive by dominating the other chicks in the nest of its foster parents.

A young cuckoo ejects the other young birds from their nest.

NOTE HOW SHORT THE TAIL IS
AT FLYING STAGE.

YOUNG SONG THRUSH CRASH LANDS

Learning to fly can be a hazardous task. A young Osprey exercises its wings; while a Song Thrush leaves the nest and crash-lands on the ground.

Gradually the chicks develop in size and grow their feathers until they are able to fly. During the days before their first outing many species exercise their wings standing on the edge of the nest and beating vigorously. But eventually they have to leave the nest and begin the most dangerous period of their lives: The first flight is a clumsy and awkward affair often ending in a crash landing in some unfortunate position.

Can young birds fly without practice?

During the first day or two after leaving the nest many young birds are picked up by well meaning children and taken to their parents or to school. In spite of all the dangers of cats and other predators, recently fledged birds stand a much better chance left where they are than they do in captivity.

What should I do if I find a young chick?

Every young chick should be left where it is found—it has not been abandoned and its parents are nearby waiting to help.

After leaving the nest and having survived its first flight the young bird continues to be fed by its parents until it is able to care for itself. Some youngsters like the shearwaters, however, are fattened up by their parents and then deserted even before their first flight. Young Manx shearwaters spend several days alone in their nesting burrows before they emerge under cover of darkness to glide away to the sea. These young shearwaters have to learn to fly and feed themselves without any help from the adults but they are quickly able to move away and start the long migration from the shores of Britain to the coasts of South America.

What happens to the chicks once they have left the nest?

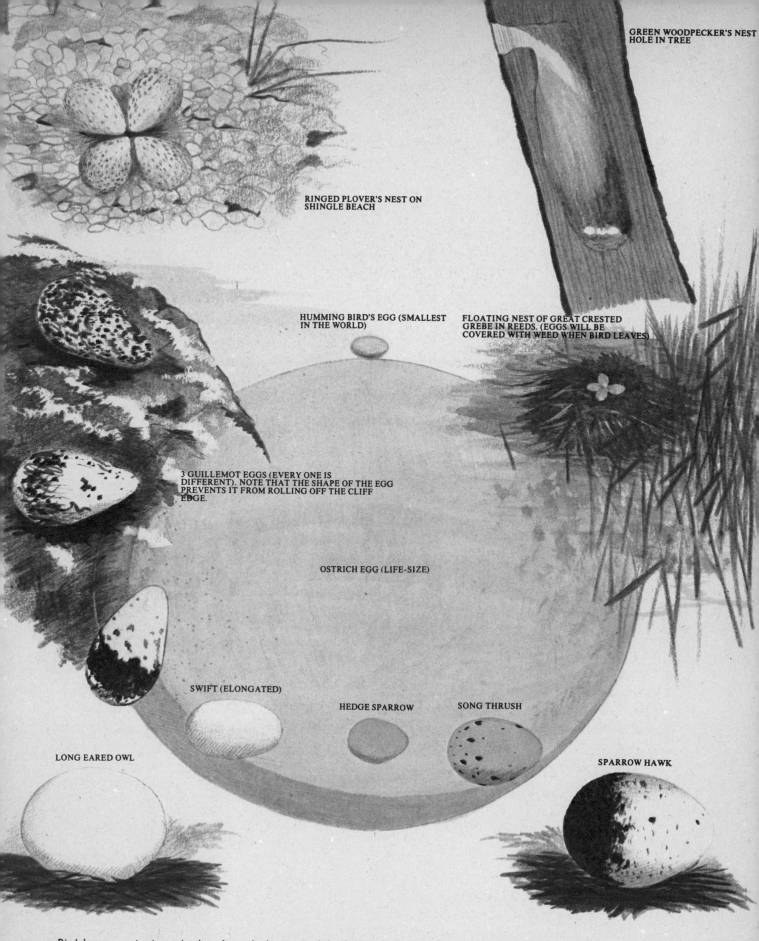

RINGED PLOVER'S NEST ON
SHINGLE BEACH

GREEN WOODPECKER'S NEST
HOLE IN TREE

HUMMING BIRD'S EGG (SMALLEST
IN THE WORLD)

FLOATING NEST OF GREAT CRESTED
GREBE IN REEDS. (EGGS WILL BE
COVERED WITH WEED WHEN BIRD LEAVES)

3 GUILLEMOT EGGS (EVERY ONE IS
DIFFERENT). NOTE THAT THE SHAPE OF THE EGG
PREVENTS IT FROM ROLLING OFF THE CLIFF
EDGE.

OSTRICH EGG (LIFE-SIZE)

SWIFT (ELONGATED)

HEDGE SPARROW

SONG THRUSH

LONG EARED OWL

SPARROW HAWK

Birds' eggs vary in size and colour from the huge egg of the Ostrich to that of the tiny Hummingbird.

33

A Peregrine swoops on a Woodpigeon.

As soon as the young are independent

Which birds form the largest flocks?

they are driven from the territory by the adults, though many birds form flocks in which they spend the autumn and winter. Small birds like finches gather in hundreds at favoured feeding grounds while some of the waders like knot and dunlin are frequently numbered in tens of thousands. The flocks feed and roost together and perform complex aerial evolutions high in the sky. Imagine a thousand birds flying at speed and suddenly changing direction together without an order being given. They wheel high overhead, dive to the land and rise up again—now showing their white underparts, now their grey backs all without a single error or crash. How they do it we still do not properly understand.

Spending their non-breeding lives

Why do birds form flocks?

together has advantages in the search for food and in protecting themselves against predators. A lone bird is easier prey to say a falcon than a densely packed flock, and when it comes to roosting the alarm call of an individual is sufficient to awaken the mass of roosting birds to any sign of danger.

Waders roost on islands among the mud

Do birds sleep together in flocks?

of estuaries where they are safe from disturbance and where they can sleep out the high tide that has covered their feeding grounds. Finches gather together in dense vegetation at dusk, while starlings often roost in reed beds, copses and on the buildings in the centre of towns. The latter are well known to city dwellers who are only too aware of the noise that vast numbers of these birds make as they rise and spiral in sky-darkening flocks over their chosen night spot.

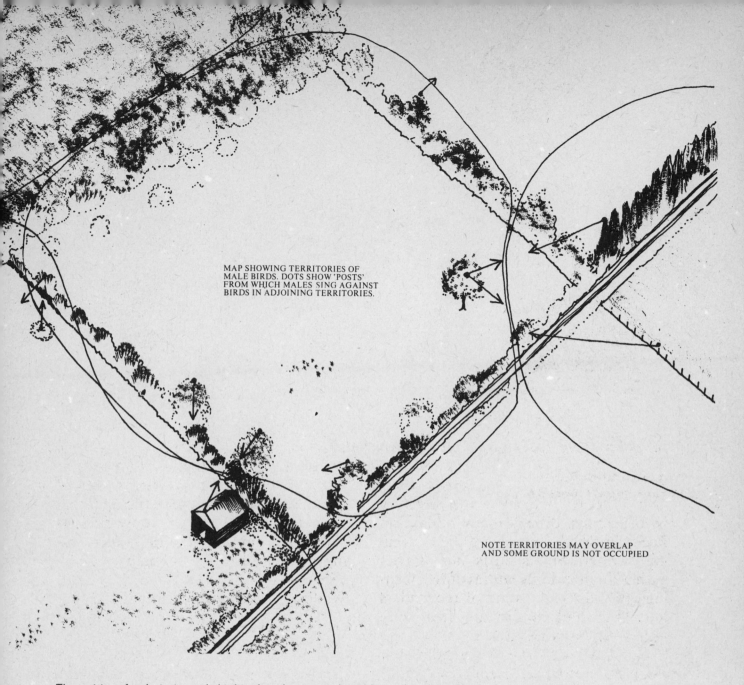

MAP SHOWING TERRITORIES OF
MALE BIRDS. DOTS SHOW 'POSTS'
FROM WHICH MALES SING AGAINST
BIRDS IN ADJOINING TERRITORIES.

NOTE TERRITORIES MAY OVERLAP
AND SOME GROUND IS NOT OCCUPIED

The position of each singing male bird is plotted on a map. Later the total number of birds can be counted.

How Many Birds

Some species have declined so far that we can actually count the individuals. There were, for instance, fifty-four whooping cranes in the world in 1970. Some other birds though many times more numerous breed only on a few isolated islands. Ornithologists

How many birds are there?

started counting the world's gannets in 1939 and produced a figure of 165,600 breeding birds for that year. Recent counts at the Ailsa Craig colony shows an increase from 5,419 pairs in 1939 to 10,402 in 1955. Other colonies show a similar increase. Just as some birds like the gannet breed in very confined areas others, that breed

35

PASSENGER PIGEON. ONCE THE COMMONEST
BIRD IN THE WORLD. (U.S.A.)

GREAT AUK. (NORTH ATLANTIC INCLUDING BRITAIN.)

Birds that have disappeared forever.

scattered over a vast area, come to-gether at a very few places to winter. The knot, for example, winters only on a few large muddy estuaries and only in extremely large flocks. By carefully counting the flocks on each estuary a total figure can be worked out. For most species, however, counting all the individuals is an impossible task. Imagine counting all of the house sparrows in a single street let alone a city.

Because we cannot count all the birds that does not mean that we cannot tell whether or not a bird is increasing or decreasing. We can simply take a sample of the birds and see what changes take place in the sample each

If we cannot count all of the birds how can we tell if a species is doing well or not?

CALIFORNIAN CONDOR (U.S.A.)

WHOOPING CRANE (U.S.A./Canada)

IVORY-BILLED WOODPECKER (U.S.A.)

Birds that are becoming extinct.

year. The British Trust for Ornithology organises a Common Bird Census in which several hundred bird-watchers scattered throughout Britain count the numbers of each different species in a small area of 50–200 acres. The smaller areas are woodland where there are a greater number and variety of birds than in the larger farmland areas. Altogether the major types of land found in Britain are covered, though there are more farms than anything else because of the greater danger of farm chemicals killing birds.

Each watcher visits his census area at least six times during the summer months and plots the position of each singing male bird on a map. At the end of the summer he takes all of his

How does a census work?

different sitings of a single species made at different times, and plots them on a single map. This will show him exactly where he saw a great tit for example every time he went to his area. He can then see from the pattern just where the territories of each bird are and thus how many great tits there are altogether. He obtains a perfectly good result just by putting down singing males but the map can be made clearer if he also puts down nests when he finds them and the flight paths of birds when he disturbs them. His final total is checked by experts at the Trust and a final picture of how many pairs of birds there are of every species that occurs in his area emerges.

If the census worker keeps up his observations every year an index of population is built up. This means that he will be able to say that willow warblers are more plentiful this year or that wrens are well down on what they were before. If the results from all the census areas from different parts of the country all show a similar increase or decrease we

Does the census worker have to visit his area every year?

can see how any particular bird is doing—not only interesting information but possibly vital to conservation.

By and large the numbers of most birds remain roughly stable, but some fluctuate remarkably over a five or six year period. In Europe and North America waxwings, crossbills and nutcrackers come into this group. Breeding in the far north the number of these birds that survive the winter depends on the quantity of seeds produced by the trees that they feed on. Waxwings eat rowan and other berries, crossbills eat the seeds from pine cones, and nutcrackers crack seeds and nuts. If there is a very good crop of seeds then large numbers of birds will survive the Arctic winter to breed the following summer. There will then be huge numbers of young birds in the autumn which is all right if the seed harvest is exceptionally large but a disaster if there is only a normal crop. If this happens birds leave southwards in search of food in vast flocks appearing in places where they never occur normally. These movements are called irruptions.

What is an irruption?

Irruptions occur when flocks have to search for food in areas of the world where they do not normally go.

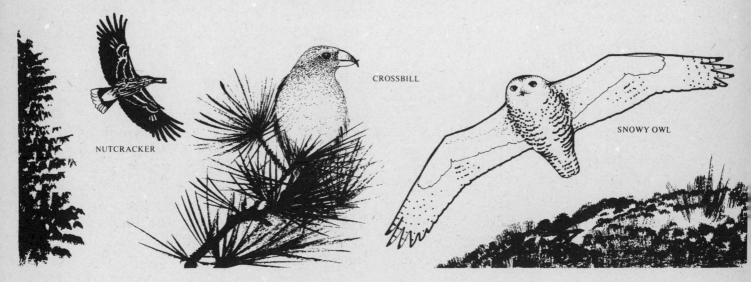

NUTCRACKER

CROSSBILL

SNOWY OWL

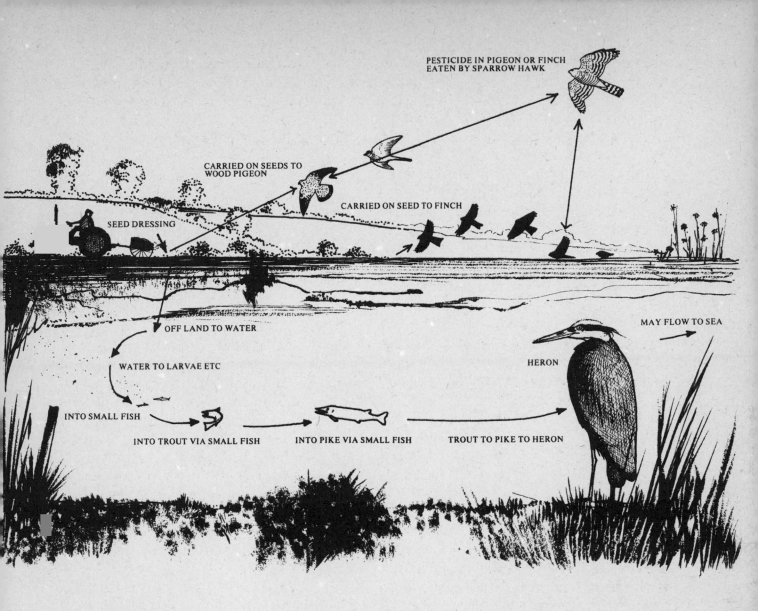

PESTICIDE IN PIGEON OR FINCH
EATEN BY SPARROW HAWK

CARRIED ON SEEDS TO
WOOD PIGEON

CARRIED ON SEED TO FINCH

SEED DRESSING

OFF LAND TO WATER

WATER TO LARVAE ETC

MAY FLOW TO SEA

HERON

INTO SMALL FISH

INTO TROUT VIA SMALL FISH   INTO PIKE VIA SMALL FISH   TROUT TO PIKE TO HERON

Spraying crops to kill insects creates an uncontrolled chain of killing ending with the larger rare predators.

Birds and Man

Men and birds have lived side by side **When did man become a real menace to birds?** for over a million years but it is only in the last five hundred or so years that man has had any real effect on them. As soon as man began to explore the world in the sixteenth century he began to introduce animals into places they had never been before. Imagine an island on which no man had ever set foot before. It is covered with nesting birds – perhaps several million of them. Then a galleon lands in the bay and men come ashore. They have had no fresh food for months and they take

LIVE GUILLEMOT COMPLETELY OILED

DEAD

GUILLEMOT   BLACK-HEADED GULL

OPERATION   SEABIRD

RESCUERS AND VAN.

VERY BADLY OILED BIRDS WILL BE
KILLED (THEY WILL DIE ANYWAY).
PARTLY OILED BIRDS ARE CLEANED
IF POSSIBLE AND ARE KEPT UNTIL
NATURAL OIL RETURNS TO FEATHERS.
RECORDS OF OILED BIRDS ARE KEPT.

LIVE GUILLEMOT PARTLY OILED

RESCUE

many eggs and birds to eat, but more important are the rats that have lived in the ship's holds and which find the nesting birds a feast when they come ashore. Later men settle on the island and find the rats such a pest that they introduce cats to deal with them. This sounds bad for the rats but the cats find an easier living feeding on birds too. At Ascension Island, a speck in the middle of the Atlantic Ocean, this happened and most birds now survive only on a tiny offshore rock called Boatswain Bird Island. But similar tories could be told all over the world.

What are the results of using farm chemicals?

In the last 500 years about 94 different species of birds have become extinct and a further species disappears every few years or so. Today the main problem is that there are just too many people polluting the planet. On the land we use more and more chemicals many of which are harmless and enable us to produce more food, but some of which are lethal to birds and perhaps to us eventually. Because we take so much out of the land we are having to put more and more back in

CHAFFINCH

BLACKBIRD

BITTERN

MARSH HARRIER

AVOCET

Bulldozers remove hedges to make larger fields destroying Chaffinch's habitat. Marshes are drained and Bittern, Marsh Harrier and Avocet are made homeless.

GUILLEMOT   RAZOR-BILL   PUFFIN

RED-THROATED DIVER   EIDER

GULL   SWAN

Oil pollution affects many birds.

the form of fertilizers, but these are washed away by rain and are concentrated in lakes that quickly become overgrown and of no use to birds that need open water. Hedges are removed, ponds are filled in, marshes are drained and forests cut down to be replaced by plantations. Every act takes away some place where a bird could live and nest in safety.

Oil in the sea kills thousands of birds – will seabirds eventually become extinct?

Oil tankers dump oil at sea and even with new methods of cleaning their tanks they still have accidents that discharge hundreds of thousands of tons of filthy greasy crude oil into the sea. Beaches are covered and thousands of seabirds die an agonized death as they become waterlogged. Puffins, razorbills and particularly guillemots are frequent victims and there is no doubt that the number of these birds is seriously declining in northern Europe.

AQUATIC

SWALLOW

BLACK VULTURE

BLACK BROWED ALBATROSS

DESERT BIRDS

HOUBARA BUSTARD

PALLAS'S SANDGROUSE

HOOPOE-LARK

FOREST BIRDS

SCARLET TANAGER (AMERICA)

BANDED KINGFISHER (S.E. ASIA)

RUBY & TOPAZ HUMMING BIRD
(CENTRAL S. AMERICA)

WATER BIRDS

BLACK WINGED STILT

SABINES GULL

SHOVELER

SHOVELER (MALE)

EMPEROR PENGUIN

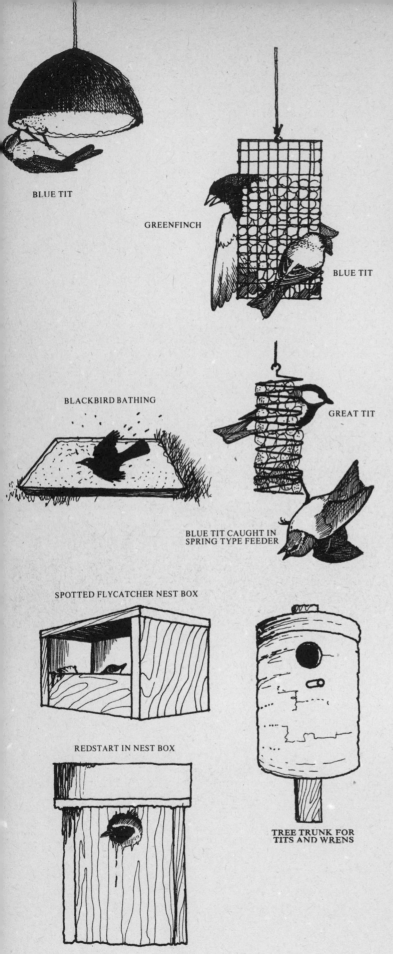

BLUE TIT

GREENFINCH

BLUE TIT

BLACKBIRD BATHING

GREAT TIT

BLUE TIT CAUGHT IN
SPRING TYPE FEEDER

SPOTTED FLYCATCHER NEST BOX

REDSTART IN NEST BOX

TREE TRUNK FOR
TITS AND WRENS

Do people still shoot and trap birds? Some countries still allow wild birds to be caught and put in cages while others even allow small garden birds to be shot to eat. Even in Britain where it is illegal to shoot any bird without authorization and where most birds are totally protected at all times, there is still a great deal of illegal shooting, trapping, and egg collecting. Even more important there is no law prohibiting foreign birds, except eagles, hawks and falcons, from being brought into the country and being sold. This export business is very damaging to the birds of many parts of the world.

Are men always the enemies of birds? The story of man and birds is not all bad, however. With more and more people like yourself becoming interested in birds there are fewer and fewer shooters and egg collectors. There are more nest boxes, bird baths and garden feeders available. If you join societies there is more money available to buy bird-reserves where experts can look after the birds' needs, and more pressure on responsible governments to preserve nature.

FEEDING TABLE

All you need to start bird-watching is

What do I need to become a bird-watcher? an identification book and a pair of binoculars, head for the local common or open space and start watching. Later you may become really keen and get all of the equipment to enable you to pursue your hobby come rain, storm or snow.

A variety of equipment can be used for birdwatching from an identification guide to a telescope.

FIELD GUIDE

NOTE BOOK

BIRD LIST

TELEPHOTO LENS

CAMERA

BINOCULARS

TELESCOPE

TAPE RECORDER

MIST NET
(FOR REGISTERED RINGERS)

MIST NET SUPPORTS

MALE BULLFINCH. FOUND IN GARDENS,
HEDGEROWS AND WOODS.

BLUE TIT. FOUND IN GARDENS
AND WOODS.

ROBIN.